HOW TO PERSUADE PEOPLE

(and get what you want)

ROB ALCRAFT

Heinemann Educational Publishers
Halley Court, Jordan Hill, Oxford OX2 8EJ
a division of Reed Educational & Professional Publishing Limited

Heinemann is a registered trademark of Reed Educational & Professional Publishing Limited

OXFORD   MELBOURNE   AUCKLAND
JOHANNESBURG   BLANTYRE   GABORONE
IBADAN   PORTSMOUTH (NH) USA   CHICAGO

© Rob Alcraft, 1999

The moral right of the proprietor has been asserted.

First published 1999

03 02 01 00 99
10 9 8 7 6 5 4 3 2

British Library Cataloguing in Publication Data
A catalogue record for this book is available from the British Library.

ISBN 0 435 09677 X   *How to Persuade People (and get what you want)*
                            single copy

ISBN 0 435 09678 8   *How to Persuade People (and get what you want)*
                            6 copy pack

Acknowledgements
Photo on pages 4-5 reprinted with kind permission of D, P & A. Sarah Tyack,
page 6. Letter to Angela Eagle, page 9; Friends of the Earth poster, page 11;
letter to the Guardian, page 13 reprinted with kind permission of Sarah Tyack.
Dan Douglass, page 14. Radio script, page 17; Alberto Culver / Andrew Collinge
Styling Solutions advert, pages 18-19; World Vision UK / 24 Hour Famine
poster, pages 20-21 all reprinted with kind permission of World Vision. Diana Organ,
page 22. Letter to House of Commons, page 25; Westminster View news article,
page 27; extract from Hansard report, page 29 reprinted with kind permission of
Diana Organ.

**Special thanks to Sarah Tyack, Dan Douglass and Diana Organ for their
valuable contributions to this book.**

Designed by Traffika
Printed and bound in the UK

Contents

The art of persuasion

How would a bun full of worms – like the one in the picture – persuade anyone of anything? This book – I promise – will help you find out.

Did you notice I just made you a promise? I offered you the chance to find something out. I tried to get you interested.

When you try to persuade people, you too need to get them interested. And you need to offer or give them something. That could mean giving them information, or facts. You could offer them support, or a favour if they help you.

For instance, you could say, 'Mum, can I watch TV all night? I'll do the washing up for a whole month.' Or 'Let me have some of your crisps. I will always give you some of mine.'

As long as what you ask is reasonable, and what you offer is believable, then you have a good chance of getting what you want.

There are three people in this book whose jobs are to persuade people. There's an advertiser. He persuades people to buy or do things. There's a politician. She persuades people to agree with her, and vote for her. There's an environmental campaigner. She persuades people to think and act differently.

The three of them use many tricks to persuade people. You can decide for yourself whether what they do works. That bun full of worms, for instance. Is it making your mouth water?

This is a strange picture. It is meant to be. It is designed to get attention. The picture was used as part of an advertising campaign, and you can find out more about it later.

The environmental campaigner

This is Sarah. Sarah works with Friends of the Earth. Friends of the Earth is a group that tries to protect the environment. It persuades the government, businesses and ordinary people to do things that are good for the environment. It is known as a campaign group. Sarah's job is to campaign about forests.

Sarah says...

'I have to persuade people all the time – it's my job. The thing I like most is working with the media – talking to newspapers, and the radio and TV. You have 30 seconds to get across to thousands of people why forests matter so much. That's job satisfaction – completely!

'When you're trying to persuade someone, you have to break your ideas into bite-sized pieces. And you have to constantly aim your words at who you're talking to. For instance, if it's a newspaper, you have to remember you're trying to get them interested in your story. You have to do that, or they won't print it!

'Writing to a government minister is different. They're not going to be happy with punchy newspaper headlines. They want good information; they want research and facts.

'The speaking-to-people part of my job I find easy. But the writing part I've really had to work at – it doesn't come naturally to me. To help me I say to myself: "What is the main point of what I'm trying to write?"'

Persuasion: Sarah's top five tips

1. **know who you're writing to**

2. **keep to the point**

3. **make it exciting**

4. **know your facts**

5. **tell the truth**

Who are you writing to?

Government ministers are busy people. They get hundreds of letters every day. When they get another letter they must think, 'Oh no. More work, more reading.'

Sarah knows this. When she writes to a minister, she makes her letter simple and to the point. She thinks of who she is writing to – not just what she is writing about.

Sarah's letter to Angela Eagle, a government minister, is on the page opposite. She gives her letter a title so the minister can quickly see what the letter is about.

Sarah has also made sure her argument is backed up with facts and information – with evidence. 'Friends of the Earth have a reputation for telling the truth, and for not exaggerating,' says Sarah. 'We keep our reputation by doing our research, and knowing our facts.'

But Sarah does not include long reports as part of her letter. This would be boring, and get in the way of her argument. Instead she mentions them, and sends them with the letter as evidence. The minister then knows this letter is about facts that lots of other people agree with. This makes Sarah's letter more effective.

Friends of the Earth

This paragraph briefly explains what the letter is about.

This comment states that the government has not done what it said it would do. Sarah hopes to shame the minister into action by pointing this out.

Evidence is included to support the argument and make it believable.

This is a clear statement of what action Sarah wants the minister to take.

Angela Eagle, MP
Parliamentary Under-Secretary
Department of the Environment
Eland House
Bressenden Place
London
SW1E 5DU

22 May 1998

Dear Ms Eagle

Government policy and Brazilian mahogany wood

In July 1997 the government bought Brazilian mahogany for work on ships. Friends of the Earth is extremely concerned. The government did say it would think about what was good for the environment before it bought anything.

The wood came from a tree-logging company called Juary. Friends of the Earth has evidence that Juary cut down trees illegally. For your information I enclose our report 'Plunder for Profit' which mentions Juary as one of the many logging companies which have engaged in illegal logging.

All mahogany coming into the UK from Brazil comes from trees cut down in the rainforest. This is having a devastating impact on the forest and its people.

We urge you to stop all government departments from buying Brazilian mahogany, and to ensure that all wood purchased comes from a legal source that doesn't destroy the environment.

I look forward to hearing from you.

Yours sincerely

Sarah Tyack

Sarah Tyack
Rainforest Campaigner

Letter from Sarah to the government minister. Ministers make important decisions and they get many letters asking them to do things.

Bad *guy*, **good** *guy*

A lot of films and stories have a 'baddie'. There are two things we know about baddies: they are wrong, and they need to be stopped. A good guy, on the other hand, always does the right thing.

When organisations try to persuade people, they try to make themselves look like the good guy. They try to make anyone who disagrees with them look like the baddie.

Friends of the Earth is very good at the good guy, bad guy trick. A poster they used in their campaign about mahogany wood is on the page opposite. It suggests that anyone who cuts down mahogany trees or buys mahogany wood is killing people and destroying forests. They are the 'bad guys'.

'Our campaign took a hard line,' says Sarah. 'We had evidence of illegal tree cutting, and violence against the Indians who lived in the forest. In our campaign we used hard-hitting words, words like "murder".'

Using emotive words – such as 'murder' – is all part of making an issue seem a simple case of right and wrong. And people always want to be on the right side.

Friends of the Earth poster used in their campaign about mahogany wood.

"People are **dying**, the forests are **disappearing**, time is **running out**. Please stop this trade. Please stop it now."

Extract from open letter from the Amazon Working Group to the British People.

Forest peoples are threatened by the mahogany trade.

Friends of the Earth

This poster uses the 'good guy, bad guy' trick to persuade its readers. To be a good guy, all you need to do is agree with the message of the poster.

The poster uses words that someone has actually said to give it authority.

Emotive language is used to give a sense of urgency.

Everyone likes a good story

Getting a letter published in a newspaper is an effective way of getting your message or viewpoint to a wider audience. Just as in a good story, a letter giving an opinion needs to have a strong opening, a detailed middle and a conclusion.

Sarah has written a strongly-worded letter to the *Guardian* newspaper. In it she expresses her opinion of the actions of the Timber Trade Federation. This letter works very well for the newspaper. The strong language makes people think about the issue. It may prompt them to write to the newspaper to agree or disagree with Sarah. In newspaper terms, this letter is a good story. For their letters pages they want strong opinions, they want something for people to think about and perhaps respond to.

But if Sarah sent this as a private letter to the Timber Trade Federation, it would not persuade them. They would think she was rude, and would probably ignore her. Letters written like this only work if you want them to be published. Private letters must be polite, or they will not persuade anyone.

Letter published on the letters page of the Guardian *newspaper.*

Stop Rainforest Destruction

The Timber Trade Federation claims (Letters, August 1) that it has a deal with Brazilian loggers to stop damage to the rainforest. This is not true.

This deal is misleading. It is propaganda. Tree loggers claim they don't cut down trees illegally. But there is independent and reliable evidence to show that most mahogany from the Amazon is illegally produced.

Friends of the Earth is keen for people to use wood that doesn't destroy the rainforest. So we support the Forest Stewardship Council. They provide independent evidence of whether trees are cut down legally or illegally.

Does the Timber Trade Federation like this? Not much, it seems. They say their wood is just as forest-friendly as Forest Stewardship Council wood. We doubt this very much.

People have a choice when buying wood. We think that choice is an easy one to make.

Sarah Tyack
Forest campaigner, Friends of the Earth, London

The advertiser

This is Dan. Dan is a writer. He works with an advertising agency in London. He writes the words and headlines that you see in magazine adverts, or on TV.

Dan says...

'I write adverts that persuade people. I persuade them to buy something, to think something, or to do something.

'All my work starts with a brief. A brief is a list of questions and answers that tell you all about the thing you're trying to sell or persuade people about. It also tells you who you are trying to persuade, and what exactly it is you want them to do. You have to know these things before you start writing.

'When you write you need to catch people's attention. Then you have to keep them interested. You've got to choose the right words. And you have to use your imagination. It's like telling a good story – telling it well and telling it simply.

'Good writing is not just about technique. You must be clear about why you are writing. So first decide on the story you want to tell, and then go ahead – tell it. Go ahead and write.'

Persuasion: Dan's top five tips

1. **decide who you are trying to persuade**

2. **be clear about your aims**

3. **choose your words carefully**

4. **use your imagination**

5. **go ahead – write**

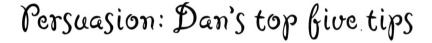

⊚ Attention!
Making people notice

Adverts are everywhere – on TV, on the bus, in the shop. You see hundreds every day. The adverts that work best are those that get your attention, and that interest you.

A script for one of Dan's radio ads is on the opposite page. It is trying to persuade young people to find out about courses at the University of Greenwich.

'Imagine what a bath full of live eels sounds like,' says Dan. He used strange sounds like this in his advert. 'The advert stood out from the everyday clutter on the radio,' says Dan. 'With advertising you need to be dramatic and punchy, or what you say will get lost among everything else.'

What Dan says about advertising is true for writing a letter. It helps to be different – then what you write will be noticed. 'But you do need to think about who you're writing to, and make what you say relevant,' says Dan.

Dan has also used humour in his advert. 'Choosing a university course could be quite scary,' he says. 'Making the audience laugh cuts through the fear about choosing a course.'

A script for actors to read. It was used as a 30 second advert on radio.

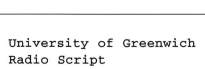

University of Greenwich
Radio Script

Some people will do anything to get
on the airwaves. Here's the pick of this
week's 'hopefuls'.

Sally kissed an old aged pensioner -
without his dentures. Sick or what?

Mike tucked into a worm sandwich.
Not exactly cream cheese and chives,
is it Mike?

And Rod settled back for a long soak
in a bath full of live eels. Nice one, Rod.

Fortunately getting on a course at the
University of Greenwich is a lot easier.
There's a lot more point to it.

And you won't have to suck up to anyone.

For your prospectus, a Guide to the
University of Greenwich, call Freephone
0500 300 195, now.

That's Freephone 0500 300 195.

Dan used a well known TV personality to read his advert on the radio. Many people know him – so they are more likely to listen to him.

This part of the advert tells people what they have to do. The writing is very clear. Persuading people is all about making sure they know exactly what they have to do.

⦿ Leave it out!
Choosing your argument

In Britain we buy tonnes of shampoo, conditioner and hair gel every day. With this much hair care on offer, persuading people to buy your product, rather than someone else's, is difficult. This was Dan's problem. His advert (which was also made into a TV commercial) is on the page opposite.

Notice what is in the ad, and what is not. The products are aimed at women. So there is a picture of a woman, with a hair style that looks good.

'You can have hair like this' is the ad's message. Dan says it worked: 'People have been to the hairdresser and actually ripped these ads out of a magazine, and said "I want that look."'

But Dan has left something very important out of this advert. He has left out the price. 'We're trying to create a mood with this advert. We want people to feel something, and aspire to the look we create. It's not about price.' What Dan has done is chosen his argument, and stuck to it.

Magazine advert for Andrew Collinge Styling Solutions. One page can cost hundreds – or thousands – of pounds, so the ads need to work well to be worth it.

Applying style to haircare is where Andrew Collinge excels. Through his regular TV appearances, on-screen makeovers and award successes, Andrew has become the leading light in British hairdressing. He's now brought that sense of style to his state-of-the-art Styling Solutions product range – designed to create any style you choose and keep it. Andrew Collinge Styling Solutions contain special style and shine enhancers that

Before

no holds barred

andrew collinge styling solutions will create the hold you want so you can create the look you want

control your hair, protecting against style collapse every time. From the Moussing Gellé to the Finishing Hairspray, Styling Solutions combines maximum flexibility with maximum hold for a look that lasts every time. For everyone who wants to take control, there is a Styling Solution by Andrew Collinge.

andrew collinge

styling
SOLUTIONS

DESIGN & SHINE – GEL SPRAY – FINISHING HAIRSPRAY – MOUSSING GELLÉ – STYLING WAX

What's the problem?

Structuring your argument

Some advertising that Dan writes does not offer the person reading it anything at all. It just gives them the chance to feel like they have done the right thing. This sort of advertising is mostly for charities.

'It's all about giving someone the idea that they can do something,' says Dan. The ad on the opposite page is for the charity World Vision. It sets out the problem – a worm that lives inside people's bodies – very clearly. The ad also uses a picture of the Guinea worm wound round the page to give a visual image of the problem.

Then Dan's ad tells readers what they can do to help. First it states the problem, then what people can do about it. Using this structure makes the writing clear, and easy to understand. It lets people concentrate on what they are being asked to do.

It is important too, to phrase the help wanted in the right way, to make it sound easy. 'We've broken down the action we want people to take into a measurable unit of time, into 24 hours,' says Dan. There is no doubt about what is being asked. It does not seem much. Already the reader is halfway to being persuaded.

An advert for a charity event. It appeared in pop and fashion magazines for young people.

...yanyiik has to drink water through a filter pipe

worms will grow inside her

Eleven year old Nyanyiik Magac lives in southern Sudan in Africa.

In her village the only drinking water is filthy and often contains the eggs of the Guinea worm. These eggs hatch and grow up to one metre in length (like the worm shown on this page) and live in the intestines. After a year the worms break through the body, usually out of the legs or feet, causing unbelievable pain. Often the victims are unable to work or plant crops, which can lead to food shortages.

Nyanyiik has already suffered from one of these worms, and it was removed without anaesthetic. Now she has another Guinea worm inside her.

❝ I'm scared because I know there's another worm in my foot which still has to come out and I remember how painful this was last time ❞

To avoid more Guinea worm eggs entering her body, Nyanyiik has to drink water through a filter pipe, which is shared by several families.

By taking part in the 24 Hour Famine on 20th March and going without food for 24 hours, you'll be helping World Vision provide filter pipes to stop people swallowing Guinea worm eggs. You'll also help to provide immunisation and health clinics to treat people suffering from Guinea worm.

Could you go hungry for just 24 hours to help someone like Nyanyiik? If so, send for your FREE 24 Hour Famine kit today.

...in your life
...akes to help
...like Nyanyiik

WORLD VISION
Practical Christian Caring

24 HOUR

Tel no _____
E-Mail Address _____
Return to: 24 Hour Famine,
FREEPOST MK1730,
Milton Keynes, MK9 3YZ.

Or, if you live in Eire: 24 Hour Famine,
10 Main Street, Donnybrook,
Dublin 4.

JB981N

21

The politician

This is Diana. Diana is a Member of Parliament, or MP for short. She was chosen by the people, or constituents, of the Forest of Dean to speak for them in Parliament.

Diana says...

'Being an MP is really two jobs. First there's the Parliament bit – where I go Monday to Thursday night. Last week we worked through the night, to do urgent work. I arrived at 3 o'clock and left at 9 o'clock the next morning.

'Very often I have to talk to groups of people and persuade them of a point of view. Most nerve-racking of all is speaking in Parliament. It's terrifying! When I was speaking in a debate on beef, I had all the opposition baying at me. They weren't going to let me have an easy time. They were trying to pull me apart, laughing at me, shouting at me, and giving abuse. It is very, very intimidating!

'Then the other bit of my job is in the Forest of Dean. I go to meetings, village halls; I talk to business people, councillors – everybody. And I have to be seen out and about. Sometimes I have to face public meetings of 800 people, all of whom are a little unhappy!

'I persuade people – but I also get people trying to persuade me. If what someone says or writes is clear, then it can work. If they waffle, then I end up not knowing what they want me to do.

'When I persuade someone, I try never to be too emotional, or go over the top. I always try to be sincere and passionate.'

Persuasion: Diana's top five tips

1. give people the facts

2. say what it is you want

3. use clear, simple language

4. be passionate, but not emotional

5. repeat your argument

Make it short, make it clear

Diana's office writes and sends hundreds of letters every day. She does not have time to make them long letters. Nor do the people who read them want to spend ages reading a long letter. Diana keeps her letters short and to the point.

Diana wrote the letter on the page opposite. It is about a man who wants to remain in his caravan home. 'I often speak on behalf of my constituents,' says Diana. 'They are a small voice against big organisations. I use the fact that I'm an MP to say "Come on, do something, get something sorted out!"'

There are just three paragraphs in the letter. Diana has used only the facts that she thinks make her argument a strong one. Everything else – just like Dan and his hair care ad – she leaves out.

'Keep things simple,' says Diana. 'Simple words and language can be very persuasive.'

Diana was asked to help one of the people in her Forest of Dean constituency. This is the letter she wrote to try and help them.

Before we even read the letter we know where it is from, who it is for, and what it is about.

Mr C J Shaw
Borough Planning Officer
Tewkesbury Borough Council
Gloucester Road
Tewkesbury
Glos
GL20 5TT

18th May 1998

Re: <u>Mr Weston and the Council's Housing Structure Plan</u>

Dear Mr Shaw

I write on behalf of Mr Weston who is one of my constituents. He has told me of his problem of the right to live permanently in his caravan home. Mr Weston has been told that his home does not fit the Council's Housing Structure Plan for the area.

Mr Weston and his family have lived in Ashcroft Road for nine years. To my knowledge they have never caused trouble, nor had complaints made against them. Making them move would cause distress and unhappiness. I do not believe that this is the right solution.

I would be grateful if you would reconsider your decision, and include Mr Weston's caravan site in the Structure Plan. I do feel that it would be right to show flexibility in this case.

Yours sincerely

Diana Organ

Diana Organ MP
Forest of Dean

The letter uses formal language. This can make your letter seem well thought out, sensible and important.

Each paragraph does one job, and one job only. Using paragraphs like this is an easy way to structure an argument. Paragraphs work well as little bites of information. At the end of each paragraph people have a chance to breathe. Then they are ready for the next bite of information.

◎ **Asking questions**
you don't want answered

Do you ever ask questions you do not need answers to? Diana does. They are called rhetorical questions. The point of using these kinds of questions is that the answers are obvious. The answers should support your point of view, and help you persuade.

Diana uses rhetorical questions in her newspaper article on the opposite page. 'I'm allowed to put anything I like into my newspaper column,' says Diana. 'I talk about anything controversial, and I try to get people to think, and write in.'

Look at the question at the end of the second paragraph: 'Are all these car journeys really necessary?'. We all know that the answer is, 'No, probably not'. But Diana is not asking this question to get an answer. Instead she wants people to think about how much they use their cars and how often they could use the bus, or walk, instead.

Diana writes for her local newspaper once a week. Here is one of her articles from July 1998.

26

Wednesday, 22 July,1998

Westminster View

How easy is it for us in rural areas to use our cars less? The Transport White Paper announced this week is challenging all of us to think about whether all our car journeys are really essential. Something has to be done about urban congestion. We cannot allow the continual increase in car journeys to end in complete gridlock.

One of the major causes of congestion is the school run. Parents do have genuine fears about safety. So highlighting safe routes for children to walk or cycle to school will help to ease traffic at peak school journey times. I am amazed at how many children are dropped off at school in cars. Are all these car journeys really necessary? Shouldn't children be able to walk or cycle to school?

But I do accept that it is difficult in rural areas. Many children have to travel long distances to school, often along lanes that are not really safe for younger children to walk or cycle on. Because of the lack of decent public transport many parents now drop their children off at school and then travel on to work by car.

It may not be as easy for people in rural areas to cut down on car use as it will be for those in cities. But I do believe that we also have a responsibility to think about whether our journeys are really necessary. We should be organising school runs with other parents. We could cut the number of cars by half. When children walk or cycle they become healthier and fitter. What do you think? Can we cut down on school journeys in rural areas?

◎ If it's worth saying once, Say it again

Next time you hear a politician speaking on the TV or radio, listen to what they say. You will notice that very often they say the same thing, again and again. Repeating yourself when you talk to friends would be boring. But when you are trying to persuade someone it can help to underline your argument.

'Politicians repeat themselves on purpose,' says Diana. 'When you talk to an audience, they don't listen to you all the time. So you repeat the main point of your argument, so that people will remember it.'

Diana has been taught to repeat herself, especially when she is talking on the radio. 'I was even taught to ignore the interviewer's question,' says Diana. 'Say the three things you want to, and then repeat them.'

When Diana speaks in Parliament she uses the trick of repeating her most important points – just to make sure that people notice and remember them. On the opposite page are some parts of a speech she gave in Parliament. The speech was about poor people living in the countryside. One of the main points she is making is that public transport is very important in the countryside, so she mentions this several times.

House of Commons

Wednesday 4 February 1998

Rural Poverty

Poverty in cities is easy to see. We all see it, in high-rise flats, rough sleepers in cardboard boxes, graffiti and litter. But poverty in the countryside is hidden. Car ownership, for instance, is seen as an indication of wealth. But in rural areas owning a car is a necessity, not a luxury, because of the lack of public transport. 75% of all English parishes do not have a daily bus service. Many people in rural areas sacrifice a lot to keep the car on the road.

Seven market towns in Gloucestershire were shown in a survey to have areas of real poverty. The survey showed high unemployment, lack of job opportunities, drug and alcohol abuse problems among the young, and people isolated by inadequate transport services.

People are doubly disadvantaged when they are poor and live in the countryside because of the lack of good public transport. No transport means that they live in a no-go area: no-go to advice centres, doctors, jobs or interviews.

> **Notice how in these places Diana is repeating herself. She is making sure that people know what her argument is, and remember it.**

In Parliament, MPs sometimes get the chance to make a speech. Everything that is ever said in Parliament is written down in a book called Hansard. Here are parts of a speech, Diana made, about rural poverty.

Now you're an expert!

The three people in this book have three very different jobs. But have you noticed they all try to persuade people using many of the same tricks?

◎ They all think about who they are writing to.

◎ They all make sure they know why they are writing, and what they want to achieve.

◎ They all try to grab their reader's attention.

◎ They all try to write clearly. They keep to the point.

◎ And they all try to use their imagination when they write. They use their own words or ideas, so that what they write is fresh and original.

All the people in this book did something you are doing – they learned and practised the tricks of persuasion. Sarah – the campaigner from Friends of the Earth – admitted it was hard work. Diane – the MP – said she was sometimes terrified. And Dan – he said you just have to get on and do it.

Mr C J Shaw
Borough Planning Officer
Tewkesbury Borough Council
Gloucester Road
Tewkesbury
Glos
GL20 5TT

18th May 1998

Re: Mr Weston and the Council's Housing Structure Plan

Dear Mr Shaw

I write on behalf of Mr Weston who is one of my constituents.
He has told me of his problem of the right to live permanently
in his caravan home. Mr Weston has been told that his home does
not fit the Council's Housing Structure Plan for the area.

Mr Weston and his family have lived in Ashcroft Road for nine
years. To my knowledge they have never caused trouble, nor had
complaints made against them. Making them move would cause
distress and unhappiness. I do not believe that this is the
right solution.

I would be grateful if you would reconsider your decision, and
include Mr Weston's caravan site in the Structure Plan. I do
feel that it would be right to show flexibility in this case.

Yours sincerely

Diana Organ

Diana Organ MP
Forest of Dean

"People are dying, the forests are disappearing, time is running out. Please stop this trade. Please stop it now."

Extract from open letter from the Amazon Working Group to the British People.

Forest peoples are threatened by the mahogany trade.

Friends of the Earth

Index